IF YOU HAVE TO GO

Also by Katie Ford

Deposition
Storm (chapbook)
Colosseum
Blood Lyrics

IF YOU HAVE TO GO

POEMS

❧

Katie Ford

GRAYWOLF PRESS

This publication is made possible, in part, by the voters of Minnesota through a
Minnesota State Arts Board Operating Support grant, thanks to a legislative appro-
priation from the arts and cultural heritage fund, and a grant from the Wells Fargo
Foundation. Significant support has also been provided by Target, the McKnight
Foundation, the Lannan Foundation, the Amazon Literary Partnership, and other
generous contributions from foundations, corporations, and individuals. To these
organizations and individuals we offer our heartfelt thanks.

Published by Graywolf Press
250 Third Avenue North, Suite 600
Minneapolis, Minnesota 55401

www.graywolfpress.org

Published in the United States of America

ISBN 978-1-55597-811-2

2 4 6 8 9 7 5 3 1
First Graywolf Printing, 2018

Library of Congress Control Number: 2017953355

Cover design: Jeenee Lee Design

Cover art: Candace Jahn

Again for the theologian Gordon D. Kaufman, this time,

Somewhere—in silence—

Contents

I

In the Hearth   3

II

The Addresses   7

III

Psalm 40   53

IV

The Ready Heart   57

Iridescent Lake   58

Triolet with Two at the Hill   60

You Occurred to Me   61

All I Ever Wanted   62

Whither can the heart go from the heart—

AUGUSTINE

IN THE HEARTH

Of life's abundant confusions
this does not partake.
My body gripped stiff at length
by a smith I cannot see.

Alone, not alone, my faceless smith,
if I could speak from the forge
I'd want to beg you
not to stop, not to feel

the guilt
of your injurious labor.

I know my labor, and whatever shape
my body now is bent to,
it returns me
to that labor.

I don't think when I return
I will have a story.

Three things I shall say: I knew I was
not entirely alone;
when I could speak again
it was from a bath of cool water;

but first:
I was kept
a long time
in a flame.

⁓

And so I was scared to be in my body,
in the same way one fears a particular house.

Perhaps I should move my body, I'd think,
but movement is oftentimes prevented
though knowledge of the exact encumbrance
is not permitted.

Felt, yes,
but not defined. Contoured,
but not traceably so.

Yet my body extends itself outward—
it is now the house, the rooftop, the lake and lotus—

this is not good news, this is not beauty:
I am everywhere and the fear, when it desires
to grow, grows continental, drifting,
torn, submerged—

and so I ask my body for another house.

But the body worsens under the extremity of the request,
saddening further like corners
of a fabric sack
bearing the very most of the stones.

Whatever my body now is bent to,

I don't want to have a story.

II 5

THE ADDRESSES

I make my bed every morning.
I don't know where to start
so I start with the bed.
Then I fall to my knees against it.

1

Empty with me, though here I am, I saw
some soul set my meal with dream, then leave
a gift for me: a ten-toothed comb to rake what's dead
from me until the comb's carved medieval scene

where bend two horses, water-consoled,
adds to me the hope of that number.
My own comb's a lime-shined prairie
with the grass of plastic acres.

My carver never was? or must have roamed.
All I ever wanted was the communal table,
so I do love the steady hand
that carved this other comb:

the fence of the kingdom if turned tooth-side down.
The kingdom does come. For me, this is how.

2

So tiny is the kingdom come
I must weigh and work the taxed fractions
of how my soul's paltry income
might be counted in.

Love isn't mathematics? Oh yes it is.
Do you think it's a cold thing to say?
And what do I know of math? I know more than I've said,
I know nearly everything there is:

I can add and divide and feel the abstraction
subtracted. That's as critically far as any math goes.
My one hand tracing two horses is a relief geometry
I can feel. Look at them: no auction block and not alone,

not bit-yanked to the barrel where drums the beast's scared heart.
I bid all on my comb horses. Of which I'm not a part.

3

I bid on two not up for tender
at the kingdom's comb fence. You're Andalusians,
I think . . . it'd hurt too much to give you names.
Your eyes are soft to me of no choices,

even as you bend to feed.
So many foods to eat—. And one is of affliction.
I'll know more by its end or grow so scarce of myself
it won't matter what bread did or couldn't descend.

I'd rather starve than eat alone the bread of heaven.
So it's true the kingdom knows me? It let me see these horses?
There's no proof, just so much given:
animals that thirst, a river near horses.

One looks up, the other drinks down.
Beneath a red line goes the day: sundown.

4

I'm red with the hurt of sundown.
It makes me want to pull the comb through my hair.
I hear the horses quiet at the river-handle. They've grown
uneasy, shy, they're scared.

What creature could know what to say when asked,
Can I drag you through me, just to feel?
The poor horses can't recoil, whinny, or move task to task.
The question terrifies. I suppose it's real.

Still, can I—may I—drag you through me, little comb?
Boxwood, fine-grained, ancient tool—
can't I be allowed to need you, too?
Your history prescribes you a lasting need.

My history is all alone, and alone, I know,
is all. I pick up the comb.

5

I pick up the comb, but don't know where to start.
A lonely life goes lonely everywhere,
even where I plait my part. I suppose
there's no reason not to start at the scars—

surgical, homemade—all of it goes under the rake.
My skin's no stony table; the kingdom's
not come here before. My hand grips—
a mane, I think—a flank's accustomed cold.

Is this a shank? a mouth?
some teeth gone rank?
I thought I'd feel something beside me
to comb out the fright. I suppose I was right:

fright came true,
and turns on a crank.

6

I took the crank because fright, you're mine,
so dig from crown to belly.
But a tooth caught a link of necklace—
a locket, of course. This is true use:

to keep one sweet thing around the neck,
pre-forged and metal-strong.
The comb drags my Eden-sore mind
until even the God of it goes.

Why is it the kingdom yesterday sat near
and now asks excuse from my table?
I know my brand of human:
the kingdom only seems, and even that is rare.

I define rare like this:
it comes, then it goes, then it never was.

7

It comes, then it goes, then it never was.
I didn't think the kingdom was supposed to be like that.
Theologies lay and stretch me on the rack.
I didn't think love should feel like that.

I can only live through a glass, darkly.
Ask, it shall be given, I can't even try.
Half ago my life I lifted up to the mountains.
On a swim dock I sat dry as dry while

in the water rose a ragged catfish, its mouth an open glass.
Glassy water into glass-made mouth.
None of my shape opens to none that would pass
as ghost of a ghost of a right-hungry mouth.

Love lays me on the rack. My desire's all gone wrong.
It's starved. And strong.

8

I think the tradition so stupid and wrong
of mourners-for-hire (keeners who slap tambourines)
just to stuff a sad scene. The more crammed
the number, the more I see

that single girl, right over there, hook over the grave
of her own what-never-will-be.
She's not even come close. It's all a big fat miss.
She sits vigil there. I guess that's what I'd call this.

Why ever purchase more of herself—
self after self to rip out her hair,
a crowd thrashing its ribs over a grave's dank must—
I think grief's worse struck against a single chest.

I'll retch now over my ground.
Luckily nobody, not anybody's, around.

9

Luckily nobody's around
to hear me send my sick into the ground.
This is how I pray to the saint of impossible cause:
I don't call her name—

my body does it all. Not a thing do I make up:
there wasn't any honey water, there wasn't any priest.
Believe in this: a shaking body,
an indiscernible breeze.

All day, day says the kingdom doesn't care.
It's just not there, or it leaves us so long
I'll have to forget the horses of the comb,
forget they ever ran through my hair.

Look at me looking at me look at carved things
I wish I could be.

10

I wish I could leave me.
I can't even know if the horses are for me
or against me, of me or in me,
beside or despite me—

are they gods?
or mangy beasts?
were they bought by some empty patron
buying life straight into me—

I once said they were looking at me,
but that may have been the sorry glance of a shun—.
We love to read into animals,
but they might not want anyone.

They might not want anyone?
Then where's gone my kingdom—

11

All goes to gone. God of my childhood,
with your attendant monstrosities,
have a little warmth on me, bent and frozen.
Hastily now and again it seems you can hear

even the farmyard rats
gnaw at cobs and whatever fresh dead's around.
Though it's confusing to see the golden
seaport alongside all that—well, such is

the human eye that doesn't get to choose
unless it trains, and I wasn't given the gift of exercise.
I will not say you've given me a terrified silence,
nor absence, nor presence, nor the sun red and down,

whose going you can't protect. Let me,
dusky godsend, never believe you protect.

12

I believe that you destroy,
I can't that you protect.
What I mean is this: each day I receive
and, by moon, night shines to erase.

It gets dark in this world,
how can I save what's erased by day—?
Body, the good, is porous: all comes along.
I'd like even to say the body is *for* us:

I downed once the sight of a man
who swam out and in at the beach
then read between swims on the sand
clearly in repair from what was required of him.

Fine, night: erase. But I'm still made
by the sight of those swims.

13

By the sight of those swims
I'll be bound by this contract,
even if it's my sole eyes that sign.
I've done worse, and it's true,

all on earth does fall through all.
It's the *through* that's prolonged.
It's the *through* that spills.
O snow past my window now . . .

show me, dear snow,
how to make such symmetry,
how to lock lock to lock
so I feel the inside steady

enough to believe
love might stay right here —

14

Right here, don't go—
just as I've read it could be. Dead voices,
come from my bedside table now,
you're the particulate matter of me:

I'm warm, can't I grasp? It would be life.
Oh, I see. It's your turn to sleep
your words in me, and life has bodies here.
One's right over there—

I saw two, the swimmer said to me—
a mama whale offshore, her calf in need against her—
it gave me perspective.
But it didn't, *no it didn't*, I said.

The beautiful alive doesn't grant perspective.
It grants desire.

15

Desire, that zealous servant
who won't stop tending—
you want to dress yourself, you want to leave
your hair down. The busy, allover handling

must be told away to some parlor, some outer room.
It's a Victorian scene—go dress some other girl.
The house is terrifyingly spacious!
Let me stand plain, undone in this room.

I never asked desire to be so rich—
someone transfer these monies away.
It's so easy to dress myself:
a sheath over a sheath over a skin of a self.

I sent my desire for the kingdom away.
Let it come here to my room. Let it find the way.

16

Kingdom, come here to my room.
I, too, am grown paltry with surfaces,
and have been left unsoothed, and do not wish
to be understood, and am continually thinning.

The kingdom's tired. It wanted to be impossible
to the brief world, dying for just one corner
of the table and too far for the human guest to touch.
It remains an agony away and is in agony

that we have lost the far use of agony.
It's been made ridiculous.
It feels pushed together
into a thing that can be argued.

We can play that game together.
Or we don't have to.

17

We simply don't have to.
I don't want to,
you don't want to.
I'm so tired of made-up affliction.

It makes me want to shred the faces
in front of the face. I can hear you
outside the room I just made,
breathing sharply with a hook or fork

in your mouth. You've tried hard to find this room,
little kingdom—it's easy to see you've had a hard time of it, too.
You sound like someone trying to convince
someone else you're not sick. We sickened you.

And now you won't come in. Don't be stubborn—
come see what a visit could do.

18

You know what a visit could do, you do—
I hear you through the hemlock door
mumbling *I don't know what to do, to do*—
into such pain I insist you remember

she-your-daughter, Camille Claudel,
which means you can't keep resisting her sorrow.
She broke part of herself and her sculptures, too,
when Rodin banished her to one room—.

I don't know if this letter will reach you,
daily she wrote in the asylum
of sweet alyssum, a little clay for her, and screams.
Now your mumbling's stopped.

Come be one who stands mute with me
a long, plain night on a hill, very still, without reaching.

19

What of us has any reach left for reaching—
this drowned ship's log, but maybe not skin . . .
I get upset, you know—do you want us
to feel, or worse, know, we have only the human

other? or worse, we only have ourselves? or worse,
myself, my exactly empty? You're not locked out—
you're just hiding behind my door:
enormous . . . too much definition about the eyes . . .

Described, described, described, described, described.
Now it's you who can't bear to be seen as you are.
You're right, I say through the keyhole owl:
seen as you are, *I'm sorry.*

You're cowering. I'd cower, too,
under all we've made of you.

20

We've made you, but don't misunderstand:
You were you and we try words for you.
The making made a sick wreck of you—
me, too—me, too—

Did I sing, did I wrongly?—Yes.
Did I, did I wrongly want? I chose that
and I choose this: rented room, I name you
Solus Lapis—Latin for alone all gone to stone.

But if it's my room now and the kingdom's
condensed to a fine barb of pain
I've pinned into my hair for safekeeping,
it's not going to be a bloody kingdom

where I brood.
I'll make my own room, and it will be small—

21

My room is small, but not too small—
my room is green, green, succulents and sea,
the green of a peony so red it pinkens
the comb-y light-string I hang now in my room.

Not cavernous and no space to fear:
my room.
No dank closet where someone may have died
(or buckled carefully her shoes, then died).

I make my bed every morning.
I don't know where to start
so I start with the bed.
Then I fall to my knees against it.

Without knowing what I'm falling to,
no mind makes it do it, my body just falls.

22

My body falls into just one thought:
nothing's outside my door anymore. Maybe a roach.
The one I begged for is gone. Welcome to my plot:
it just happened—

but I wanted to say one more thing—
I wanted, I had one more way—
I had the thought of a thought
that'd make you stay—

it listened to me. It did just what I said.
Comes now into my chest a dearth. It feels like a grave in there.
I suppose I owe a trental now . . . thirty requiems . . .
and . . . anyway, well . . .

welcome to my plot: sing.
Without. That I can sing.

23

You without me, you without me,
three little Christmas bells chime for a coin
outside the shop inside me. "Anything will do"
is the world's loneliest philosophy.

At least in heartache, my old friend said,
I know that I'm alive. Or so the theory goes.
(Three little bells outside the shop
chime inside me.)

But it's not a theory. It's a body, my body
lowered to bed saying *goodnight, love.*
But it's just a pretend. No one's here,
and morning will come, O it opens the shop—

—one little bell, two,
two little bells, three—

24

My hope is too open, bells!
Anyone could crawl right in.
But the rats live on a terrored wheel
of hunger and hunt

so it's world-without-end
that lies alike for me:
the mammalian fish erupting through to breathe,
the ugly grub whose undergoing won't relent,

the mind spinning on just one thought, then spent.
Ah, child-in-me, remember the birds, they neither sow
nor store. Remember, yes, I remember the verse.
That's love? to remember I'm remembered?

But I wish someone wanted to have me.
There's a difference, and difference bears the wish.

25

I wish upon a collapsed comb.
Give a more troubling sight than a downed horse:
two, then, two fallen slow on that comb.
I was asking for it, setting it upright: pretending, of course.

It's not true to say they're resting, supine.
Something was coming for to get them
and it wasn't a sleep, and it wasn't a dream.
It must have been blunt, a sudden thing.

My hair is almost done showing
how light-ready the comb had loosened it.
Is it over? I ask the quiet kitchen stone. If it's gone,
can I go then, too? go from the table's unbrightening?

May I be excused?
May I go to my room—

26

It's a species of easy to go to my room.
No kingdom holds on for dear life
when it sees me walk toward the door. I was told life
held a meanness in me, an edge.

Radiance come, so quickly gone—what can I say?
I asked excuse.
Was told *you're excused*. What left do I have
that doesn't serrate my voice.

The bright and soft is gone.
Blue chimes.
Our hill.
June sun.

The kingdom's so cold . . . and it deserves to be.
What left have I to do? but cool.

27

To wake so cool scares the thought of me,
yet it's better than a soul lukewarm.
I grant this verse its truth since through its door
I might grow a new home.

Perhaps some undistinguished, sidelong place for me?
I don't need a seat at the bannered banquet—
I'd take just a boxcar, a lean-to,
I'll stand aside the tired back of a thresher's ox.

We'll be on the field-side of the fence—
O we won't mind, my ox and I,
having pulled a long, a-trampling time.
I won't goad or swat him with a pole.

Done with hauling wagons.
Gone ropes from post to horn.

28

To shoe an ox, rope it to a post by the bit.
Or throw it to the ground.
Or lash its feet to some sturdy beam of wood.
Each shoe will seem a pretty kind of half moon,

and its waning, beautiful likeness will help you
ask of the ox the labor you will. And you will.
Here's the right place to gentle the shoes off
and smell back again an earthy thing.

He's pulled a long time.
He's hauled and ploughed
by ridge and furrow.
He's been whipped down narrow market streets.

I'm going to pull on this shoe's nails, okay, my one?
It's bound to hurt some.

29

It hurts
because the shoe's a bond.
When I yank each nail, some hoof comes along.
It's okay to bellow long. Go ahead, go on.

It'll soon be done. Enough of you will remain.
No one will blame you for staring dumb at the holes.
Listen to me, if you can: I want to miss the feast.
I'd miss anything for you.

It matters nothing that we wait—
what will come to pass
will come to pass—
we'll wait and shift injuries through the grass.

Let the grass, then me, then grass again tend each hoof.
I'll wrap what the grass can't calm.

30

Done wrapping each, then fell a calm.
It seemed to promise vacancy, the void
into privacy gone. I was scared
of how long I'd have to ask

for someplace, maybe, for me.
I'm not hostile anymore, but in the world
I felt myself a pregnancy set breach,
unable to be righted or birthed as I should.

Now the animal of the gaping hooves
gathers me into what a life can become.
What hasn't happened to him
has happened to none.

I'd like to walk my ox to the gates
to show the Lord what the world has done.

31

Do you think I don't know that when I say Lord
I might be singing into the silo where nothing is stored,
where it is written low lights were confused
by skyward light and flew its bodies

as birds against walls?
Well, everyone thrashes
against a wall
in this life.

I don't know what I mean,
but I mean it. I don't know what to want,
but I want it. And when I say God
it's because no one can know it—not ever,

not at all—. It's a wall.
And it drops to the floor as I fall.

32

From this floor I think of songs to play
on the shiny lotto piano I won.
I string them out, finish them off, and
there, I'm done.

From this floor I think of songs to play
on the shiny lotto piano I won.
I make a tune in minor C (but ever so sweet)
so *there*, I'm done.

I play songs—
I bought a piano . . .
I mean I won it—
I mean I bought it with what I won . . .

from this floor I'll try to try to play
with everything good, with everything gone.

33

The floor of it all isn't gone,
so I'll break my heart against it.
Already out in my hand, badly beating,
more wall than I'd imagined, my heart—.

Once struck, I hoped to hear
a jungle sound or two—a white monkey's shriek,
a fat, fat rain, a lion's mane swifting the leaf,
an earthy quake . . .

Am I not my heart's own master?
Remember when you shyly asked a man
to give himself to you, and when he said nothing,
you knew?

Still the heart didn't break full through.
You should know better than to tell it what to do.

34

I knew better than to light light after light.
I knew—I can't recall to see candles out
and could put the house down in burning—.
What if someone asked me, then,

do you want to receive its ashes? I'd say yes,
that's the right thing . . . (but deep down I'd say no,
no ashes). To imagine the size of the box
able to hold my home, then take it into my hands

is something I promised my hands
I'd never have them do.
They argued their case atrociously well
when they gave, as evidence, *We can't.*

Yet, lighting candles—
it's how I went on.

35

By candlelight the house went down.
It's no wonder the rats won't come sleep
in my newly rented corners . . . for me, a gathering
of low creatures would be a luminous, a concordant, a *thing*.

Be slow to wish extinct the ugly
beasts. You can't know when all that's theirs
will be more than yours, when a haystack of sleep
huddled on your porch, should it come,

wouldn't make all that's alive at dawn
be the drop of four bottles in a handled box
that, while they still shake to settle,
means someone left a remnant store of himself—

a vibration, a glass ghost, a someone, an else—
and four sweet milks to drink.

36

How deeply I drink up home-catalogs day—
they shine open my diorama and teach me
to lift my tiny arms to hang the dime
as a mirrory thing upon my shoebox wall.

Here's a sunshine page that reads,
"A home expands via the wise use of mirrors
wherever you wish a window."
I've read it all, I've read, I've read so much more

than I can withstand. A home expands via the you and I—
until then, dearest dime with my spit shined,
I will lift you up, I shall—I do—
"attend to what you do not have

and thereby," thereby. Thereby
make a home.

37

Over my home I rise on a trembling
wood-and-rope bridge. Sundown comes
in light-light red, lamps hung now in my hair
alight one question into the air:

Home, I made you best I could,
please don't break again beneath me?
I beat heavily upon my life until it gave.
As for prices, I've paid and paid.

All the while I cut the tiniest chairs,
a thimble ship, rice-paper walls
and Japanese fans cut from receipts
no wider than a little girl's nail.

Upon them I drew hills of wild plum, then
a hover of birds.

38

It was the constancy of birds
I heavy leaned upon. I'll risk you
not believing to tell a little truth: I rely upon
their whereabout sound right now.

No one coming for me, I could rot here in days.
I know Simone says forge a home in the void,
it's the void wherein roams the battered
kingdom, though she wouldn't use that word,

and neither would I except it came to me
as a strange feeling at my door to show the stones
its pockets bore, to sit and tell it was once
just a word for no, some spit in the face of lords.

No matter how we try, we're no good in the void.
Not the kingdom, not I, so birds, constancies, stay,

39

stay a spell in my persimmon tree.
I'm hefting myself up so my vacancies
might quiet in your perfect neutrality.
No contingency between us, no. Intimacy

is no promise but that we're alive a little together.
At dawn you undo my bedroom silence
and my emptiness isn't,
is not all mine to tend.

It's not traceable,
but to feel its radiance
maybe is all, maybe is everything—
maybe then arrives

the dying that breaks forth, can break open,
can break your life, it will break you

                              until you remain.

III

Psalm 40

I am content because before me looms the hope of love.
I do not have it; I do not yet have it.

It is a bird strong enough to lead me by the rope it bites;
unless I pull, it is strong enough for me.

I do worry the end of my days might come
and I will not yet have it. But even then I will be brave

upon my deathbed, and why shouldn't I be?
I held things here, and I felt them.

And to all I felt I will whisper *hosanna* for goodbye.
It is sweet to think of myself, alone at that very moment,

able to say such a thing
to all that was my life,

to all that was not.

IV

THE READY HEART

Never has there been
a love on this earth
in its quiet speech
that hasn't been prepared for
by something that keeps the lamp on at strange hours—

(such hours did not feel good, neither misunderstand
nor ought you romanticize them, since they could
just barely be borne)—.

But inside of the hours a cave
became of the gutting-out
and this was not unkeenly felt
by the host body,
but was how room was made,
a persistence arrived to lightly paint
upon the cave with lines so burgundy and so golden,
so clearly purposive and so clearly indecipherable,
neither were they buffalo nor hands,
hands roaming over the horseless plains,
plains blown through by the hot breath of the buffalo,
nor buffalo touched by human hands.

Of course the human writhed
at how finely the hollow had been chiseled.

And room was made.

IRIDESCENT LAKE

After many years, it occurred to me to write of my friends,
of their long marriage,

of the woman who woke
to find an elk had laid down on their porch
to sleep like some heft of creation
ambled out from prehistoric woods,

of how no man or woman had a language evolved enough
to articulate the elk's calligraphic intricacy of heart, nor
what wish might arrive late in age, marriage-old,
under blankets worn by her blond-gray hair,
an almost-likeness of sunrise
on Iridescent Lake,

of some form of yourself you love best because it survived the pain
cornered like a dog baring its teeth under the same porch
of our elk in this story, the same porch

of the created world resting awhile
on the stoop of this marriage.

Inside, her husband spoons sticky rice
into the middle of the bowl,
displacing soup up the sides
with the equivalency pleasure teaches us is pleasure,

just as their bodies pressed the lake
edged in thimbleberry up and up
until the perimeter was thinly watered
by his body and hers, the body she kissed
and now kisses, the body she fucked and now fucks,

the body she swims to here in a hundred lakes—
Tahoe, Rainier, Iridescent—and on the Colorado Plateau
rivered as if only for them,

he who labored
to reconvene some semblance of justice for schoolchildren
so shat upon by this country of fat wolves,
she who stripped back violent thought
written by the white minds of men
for a decade, alone at the library carrel
where the heart scholared, too,
where else could it go—.

        So now we understand the tenderness
with which he spoons rice into the center of her bowl,
why she would say to anything that pains him,
you're only thin and dirty, then tend it until it is removed
by its own thickened, cleaner ability to live well
and leave her husband alone,

though it's true they've hurt each other and November hurt them both,
they said so, separately, to me: *November.*

But the elk, who had every choice in the forest,
walked out of thin Klimt birch and wild Scotch broom
to sleep at the door
where these two slept.

Opening the door to feel for the weather but to find this elk,
who wouldn't open
all of the way
to that which halts us
to begin, once again, again.

If this were a symbol, I wouldn't brave it as an elk.
It was exactly, and only, an elk.

TRIOLET WITH TWO AT THE HILL

A hundred yards from a jagged hill
Were two who stood too far apart
In a kind of pain that kept them still
A hundred yards from a jagged hill.
It might hurt, she said, as a bed, that hill,
But earth won't play some backdrop part.
She walked the yards to the jagged hill
And soon they weren't too far apart.
So light rocks slid all down that hill—
And light rocks slid, all down that hill.

You Occurred to Me

A particular light in February,
singular in the sheen of ice upon the hill,
the groundcover grain or rayless yellow,
was sent to me in a photograph by someone thinking of me then,
a man walking in hills, I occurred to him, I
occurred. To make something of me, a photograph,
a stopping by me, a sending, it was an I
who filled another's mind. Our eyes let what is good
pass in and what is unnecessary sieve through—
that's what we want, what we practice and fail—
the world passes through and one of us occurs
to another and *is*, and stays.
If this happened only once
we would presume it a miracle,
but it happens,
and it happens,
yet didn't he say,
I should send this light,
I want her to see it perpetually,
though I saw her just once at the shore.
I had just finished a terrifying, a lonesome, a passage of a month,
and she was saying (*what?*) to me from the stones,
a denizen of seals behind her
and I couldn't read her lips,
                    do you need me?
that's what I knew she was saying, there is no knowledge,
she knew this—
            who are you? there's ocean—
            can't hear you through the seals—
—that what I know
is made of salt and air,
so I sent her (*what?*) this, to an address written in air—

ALL I EVER WANTED

When I thought it was right to name my desires,
what I wanted of life, they seemed to turn
like bleating sheep, not to me, who could have been
a caring, if unskilled, shepherd, but to the boxed-in hills
beyond which the blue mountains sloped down
with poppies orange as crayfish all the way to the Pacific seas
in which the hulls of whales steered them
in search of a mate for whom they bellowed
in a new, highly particular song
we might call the most ardent articulation of love,
the pin at the tip of evolution,
modestly shining.
                In the middle of my life
it was right to say my desires
but they went away. I couldn't even make them out,
not even as dots
now in the distance.
                Yet I see the small lights
of winter campfires in the hills—
teenagers in love often go there
for their first nights—and each yellow-white glow
tells me what I can know and admit to knowing,
that all I ever wanted
was to sit by a fire with someone
who wanted me in measure the same to my wanting.
To want to make a fire with someone,
with you,
was all.

ACKNOWLEDGMENTS

To the editors of the *American Poetry Review* (Sonnets 1–20), *Freeman's* (21), the *Literary Review* (22–24), *TriQuarterly* (31–32), *Connotation Press: An Online Artifact* (33), *Ploughshares* (34–36), *Spillway* ("The Ready Heart" and "In the Hearth"), *Los Angeles Review* ("Iridescent Lake"), and the Academy of American Poets ("All I Ever Wanted"), the author offers her deep gratitude for first publishing these poems.

Sonnets 1–14 were reprinted in *John Donne and Contemporary Poetry: Essays and Poems*, ed. Judith Scherer Herz (Palgrave Macmillan, 2017).

"In the Hearth" and Sonnets 10–13 and 31 were reprinted in *Poetry International*, 2018, ed. Ilya Kaminsky.

Thank you Jeff Shotts, David St. John, Ilya Kaminsky, Katie Peterson, Allison Benis White, Martin Pousson, Jay Hopler, Emily Rapp Black, David Hernandez, Jesse Nathan, Sarah Sentilles, Harold Schweizer, Diana Goetsch, and Nikola Madzirov for editorial notes and support of this book in manuscript form.

The epigraph from Augustine's *Confessions* is here translated by the author.

KATIE FORD is the author of *Deposition*, *Colosseum*, and *Blood Lyrics*. *Blood Lyrics* was a finalist for the *Los Angeles Times* Book Prize and the Rilke Prize, and *Colosseum* was named among the "Best Books of 2008" by *Publishers Weekly* and the *Virginia Quarterly Review*. She has received a Lannan Literary Fellowship and the Levis Reading Prize. The *New Yorker*, the *Paris Review*, and *Poetry* have published her poems, and her work is also included in *The Norton Introduction to Literature*. Ford is Professor of Creative Writing at the University of California, Riverside, and lives in South Pasadena with her young daughter.

The text of *If You Have to Go* is set in Cochin. Book design by Ann Sudmeier. Composition by Bookmobile Design & Digital Publisher Services, Minneapolis, Minnesota. Manufactured by Versa Press on acid-free, 30 percent postconsumer wastepaper.